Reviewing IT in Due Diligence

Are you buying an IT asset or liability?

Reviewing IT in Due Diligence

Are you buying an IT asset or liability?

CHRISTOPHER WRIGHT & BRYAN ALTIMAS

IT Governance Publishing

IT Governance Publishing
IT Governance Limited
Unit 3, Clive Court
Bartholomew's Walk
Cambridgeshire Business Park
Ely
Cambridgeshire
CB7 4EA
United Kingdom
www.itgovernance.co.uk

First published in the United Kingdom in 2015
by IT Governance Publishing.

ISBN 978-1-84928-720-3

FOREWORD

Over the past few years there has been a re-emergence of merger and acquisition activity, both on a mega scale, with very large mergers, and on a smaller small and medium enterprise (SME) level. The increasing dependency on IT and online commerce/channels, increase of cyber security attacks and changes in development processes for new systems have increased the significance of IT within these deals. For larger organisations/deals, IT consultants are now asked to advise and assist more during due diligence reviews. At last, IT is recognised as a key component of any deal as it can be a very costly expense post-acquisition to sort out IT issues, which should have been identified during due diligence. In some instances the deal should not have gone ahead, as the cost of resolving the IT issues could make the deal too expensive.

For some this is a new area and so we have written this book to introduce some of the key IT issues. For others, with more experience, the book hopefully provides a challenging fresh insight, and maybe generates new ideas. It is important, not only for companies in the high tech industry but also for any company with an IT-based management information system, or relying on data from computer systems for information to operate and manage the business. These same systems also produce much of the information used to make decisions about the deal, including models and forecasts of future sales and costs.

There is also increasing scope for IT due diligence specialists to become involved in mergers for small and medium-sized enterprises. These organisations increasingly rely on data and IT systems, but the need for IT due diligence is often overlooked. In these cases IT professionals may be asked to provide advice, having not undertaken such reviews previously, or unlikely to do so again in the future.

When we first got involved in IT due diligence assignments we were usually asked, just before the report was due for release, to go out and 'do our stuff'. We had no clear indication of what the deal was about or the nature of the business. The result was that we would perform a standard general IT controls review asking such questions as "Is there a backup and recovery plan?", or "Does the computer room have a fire extinguisher?", or technical IT questions. As a result our findings were of little significance or benefit to the due diligence review. The report was often unintelligible containing technical details but having no relevance to the non-technical reader. For example, "the system master passwords have not been changed for more than 150 days" – to which a reasonable reader would reply "So what?" The key consideration for IT due diligence should be the same as for any other form of financial due diligence – i.e. the impact of findings on the proposed deal, either its overall viability or value. If IT security is significant to the nature of the business or the deal, the observation about passwords could be significant, otherwise it is irrelevant.

A wider approach makes the due diligence review work far more interesting for the IT consultant and provides an opportunity to have a real impact. Fortunately over recent years due diligence reviews have become more strategic and less operational. As a result there has been an increased focus on the benefits of IT to the purchaser. The due diligence team are now likely to be more interested in whether the IT is fit for purpose, and fits with their overall plan for the business.

This book aims to provide an introduction to Information Risk Management (IRM) in due diligence – looking at types of due diligence assignments, assessing whether the target's IT is fit for purpose, project risk, assessing value and Return on Investment (ROI) for IT, and solutions to assist the deal (e.g. service-sharing arrangements). It provides an overview for each area and some of the issues to consider.

Due diligence reviews present specific challenges for the IRM specialist – there are often higher levels of assignment risks and cultural issues (especially if IT is outsourced), which are often as significant as technical issues. The quality of opinion provided by IRM can impact the price and whether the deal goes ahead. There have been specific cases where IT issues have impacted the transition post-deal. Despite this the IRM specialist is often seen as a second-class member of the due diligence team – this book will help IRM professionals to make a business case for IRM involvement and help to structure the assignment and reporting.

Generally this work is new for the current generation of IRM professionals and they seek guidance as to how it should be conducted. The tools and techniques are broadly similar to those for other assignments. The main differences are how they are applied, and the style of reporting.

Chris Wright

PREFACE

This book provides an overview of IT due diligence for auditors, anyone involved in financial due diligence and other risk professionals who may not have encountered such projects before. It also provides a perspective for organisations on what auditors and risk professionals need as key stakeholders in a due diligence exercise and the sort of questions they are likely to ask. An awareness of the issues will also help those undertaking year end financial or other audits to understand the potential IT issues that may face an entity in the future, for example if stakeholders are seeking to exit, so that preparations can commence.

In due diligence projects in the FTSE 250 market it is highly probable that there will be some focus on IT and technology. The SME market due diligence projects have a high probability that IT and technology will not be looked at in much depth. This book should change the view that IT does not need to be looked at in SME Mergers and Acquisitions (M&A) and disposal projects.

It is based on our own opinions and experience. Some will read this book and disagree with some of these ideas as every due diligence project is different. If we generate some thought and discussion then our objective is achieved.

Each chapter includes tips and hints for auditors so they can adapt their style of auditing to suit each situation. We consider detailed audit requirements for each stage in the following chapters. For each main part of the process we consider:

- what are the due diligence objectives?
- what is the impact on the value of the business covered by this objective?
- what should be included and how do you go about a review?

The auditor should focus on both the key business processes and the core systems and objectives to be included in the final deliverable.

We have also included case studies to help you understand the practicalities of the issues raised.

In my experience IT due diligence assignments can be frustrating, frightening and hard work. They are never dull and are often topical and may even be the subject of national or international media speculation. The outcome is very rewarding and with hindsight the assignments are usually fun!

Bryan Altimas

ABOUT THE AUTHORS

Bryan Altimas and Chris Wright have known each other for more than 15 years. They have worked together on IT due diligence assignments in the UK and throughout Europe, often under tight deadlines and in difficult situations. At one of the Big 4 accounting firms they helped to develop a standard approach for IT due diligence, including writing manuals and running training courses.

Bryan is a Technology Risk Management professional with more than 32 years' experience. He specialises in major programme reviews including runaway projects and governance of the technology provision in both the public and private sector, providing independent views on the project to the steering committee and programme board. Where systems are not working as expected or designed, including following mergers and acquisitions, he manages investigation teams to discover what the issues are and implement effective and efficient solutions.

He has also advised organisations on the effectiveness of their technology strategy in delivering the business strategy. Increasingly strategy is influenced by compliance of organisations systems with legal and the relevant industry regulations. As businesses develop, mergers, acquisitions and divestment occur. He has also led teams performing technology due diligence in different business sectors, geographies and circumstances.

Chris is a qualified accountant and Certified Information Systems Auditor with more than 30 years' experience providing financial and IT advisory and risk management services. He worked for 16 years at KPMG where he managed a number of major Information Systems (IS) audit and risk assignments, including some very large and famous mergers and acquisitions. These included a number of IT due diligence reviews. He was head of information risk training in the UK and also ran training courses overseas including India and Iceland. He has worked in a wide range of industry sectors including oil and gas, small and medium enterprises, public sector, aviation & travel. He has recently published *Agile Audit and Governance* also available from ITGP.

ACKNOWLEDGEMENTS

We would like to thank all of those individuals and organisations that have been brave enough to let us try new ideas and approaches. Some were successful – some were not, but all were learning opportunities. These individuals include our mothers for teaching us how to seek out bargains and ask the right questions when making purchases.

Thanks also to Brian Johnson, CA, Chris Evans, ITSM Specialist and Dave Jones, Pink Elephant for their helpful comments during the review process.

This book would not have been possible without the help, encouragement and support of a number of people especially our long-term friends and colleagues Steve Connors, Mike Hughes, Jacalyn Hutchison-Connors, Martin Douglas and Jason Mitchell. Also a special thank-you for the support and patience of our partners Amanda Wright and Anita Rai Altimas.

CONTENTS

Contents

CHAPTER 1: INTRODUCTION TO DUE DILIGENCE

Overview

Due diligence is the care a reasonable person should take before entering into a transaction or agreement with someone they don't know. However, when that transaction is for large amounts of money, and could lead to the failure of an acquiring company, special care needs to be taken. Due diligence has hence come to relate to a more formal audit or investigation process for potential transactions, to confirm all material facts for the deal. These facts may relate to legal, business, financial or even information and IT issues and may impact the deal value/price or willingness to do the deal at all. In this chapter the aim is to provide sufficient background information for a full consideration of the importance of IT in due diligence. We consider:

- history and definition.
- what is it? how do you do a review?
- what could possibly go wrong?
- summary and key take-aways.

History and definition

Some say that accountancy is the second-oldest profession (no prizes for guessing the first). This may not be true, but whenever there is trade or bargaining there is always a concern by both parties to get the best deal that they can. Cavemen may have asked the question "Is a wheel worth one deer hide or two?" Certainly we know that by the Roman era the Latin phrase 'Caveat Emptor' or buyer beware was in common use. During the Middle Ages there was a need for trust among merchants, and the ability to check out whether the guy you were trusting with your valuable shipments of silk or tea was a 'good chap'. Anyone who has travelled to the Middle East will also be aware of the bartering and bargaining and the need for vigilance. We find it somewhat ironic that so much due diligence is now performed in Wall Street, deals of $bns, when the whole of Manhattan Island is thought to have been bought from the Canarsie Indians for a few dollars. Maybe the Indians should have had better advisors, although maybe so should the settlers as some historians believe the island did not belong to the Indians to sell!

We all perform 'due diligence' whenever we buy anything. It might be just checking the best before date on a box of eggs, considering whether we can buy them cheaper somewhere else or looking at their size and whether they are free range or organic. The buying decision is based on our value judgements. For bigger, higher-risk purchases we may seek advice from a knowledgeable friend – if we wanted to buy a second-hand car, for example. For even larger purchases such as a new house, purchases most of us make only irregularly, we might seek professional advice – to ensure we are not being ripped off and that the seller has the correct title for the transaction. Big businesses and other potential investors such as private equity houses, making significant investment purchases by buying other businesses are no different. The process they go through is known as due diligence. This is an audit of the potential investment, to confirm all significant facts and assumptions, conducted before entering into a contractual agreement with the other party. The process followed is usually formal as it forms the basis of any subsequent contracts or agreements.

With an increasing litigious society the process of due diligence has become more formal and legal/financial based. Some trace this growth to the American securities laws, and certainly the issuing of shares and other securities, coupled with a loss of faith and trust in securities markets, has increased the need for due diligence reviews.

Due diligence could hence be described as healthy cynicism when considering a deal, helping to understand the evidence to support the assertions behind the deal and to understand the people you are doing the deal with. It involves getting an independent third-party opinion – but this can only be an opinion and there may be other factors that the deal parties consider when deciding how to proceed. A cynical view of due diligence could be:

> "Due diligence is an expensive, secretive process, to tell you what you already know, but in a virtually unintelligible way, by someone who does not know your business and who will try to wriggle out of any liability for their advice, but could probably still be sued for large amount of money if it all goes horribly wrong."

Yes, this view is cynical, but it does give an insight into some key elements of due diligence:

Cost – Investigations can involve large teams of specialist lawyers, auditors, managers, and capital and other professionals, working long hours under very tight deadlines (all at extremely high hourly rates!). Add in the risk elements and costs go up rapidly. The cost of the investigation needs to be considered alongside the cost of the deal, the likelihood of it going ahead and the potential loss if the identified benefits are not achieved.

Confidentiality – If any of the information about the deal, in some cases even that the deal is being considered, were to be published, the share price of the companies involved could be impacted. Due diligence assignments are therefore often given project names, non-disclosure agreements and have specific rules around data rooms and use of data.

Clarity of reporting – With clear recommendations and advice, both on the deal itself and post-deal issue(s).

Facts versus opinions – Yes, the information may be known, but also it could be hidden, or misinterpreted. Experienced due diligence specialists know the right questions to ask, including requesting specific information. This can then be presented by setting out the facts and their sources in a clear format.

Business knowledge – Due diligence investigators are employed for their independence, business knowledge of the sector and specific specialisms, including IT, required by the investigation. Some of these skills are rarely available in businesses other than those routinely undertaking merger and acquisition activities. Although most clients or the acquirer may understand the business environment in which the entity operates, they may not have the context of wider risks likely to impact the entity. What is required is good communication between the client and advisors to ensure the review is focused on agreed business, including IT, risks.

1: Introduction to Due Diligence

Liability of investigators – Investigators' contracts for due diligence assignments do contain many of their own caveats, but the review can be high risk (see "What could possibly go wrong?" later).

Due diligence is hence a process to ensure decisions regarding a transaction are made on the basis of sound information and advice. By being aware of risks and issues before the deal is made, the parties can ensure contracts are based on a realistic understanding of the deal, e.g. to negotiate best terms based upon the true value of the deal to all parties. In some cases, for strategic reasons, the deal may go ahead regardless of the due diligence review. In these cases the review is more focused on gathering information and making plans for integration post-deal. Good due diligence is more than risk and compliance; it's about basing decisions, and post-deal predictions, on sound information and judgement over:

Commercial risks such as cyber security, business continuity and compliance.

Finances – Understanding the underlying financial health and performance of the business (income and expenditure, profitability, assets, tax/other liabilities and cash flows). This is to understand past performance and assess whether this is sustainable post-deal.

Business/commercial issues – Considering the market positioning of the business and its products and services, strategic and business plan assumptions and predictions.

Legality – Understanding the legal basis of the deal and what is being transacted, including assets and intellectual property, contracts, loans and pending litigation, all of which could impact the future success of the entity . Legislation may also impact the nature of the deal itself, e.g. special anti-money laundering or anti-trust considerations.

IT systems and information can be a key element of each of these. For example:

- Finances depends on accurate, complete and reliable financial data often held in IT systems.
- IT has legal, compliance and business implications.

The two most common types of due diligence review are for:

1. M&A
2. IPO (Initial Public Offering).

M&A is a wide term used to cover the strategic changes to an organisation, not just registered companies, and its ownership. It covers buying, selling, dividing and combining of different entities. It can be confusing as to whether a change is a merger or an acquisition, especially in some cases where the brand or name of the company acquired is used as the name for the new organisation.

An IPO is the process by which a company sells its shares, on a securities or stock exchange, to the public for the first time. These have become famous in recent years with some of the large '.com' companies listing and immediately making large gains (or in some cases losses). Their purpose is to raise capital, and/or to release funds for previous investors. After the IPO the shares of the company are traded on the relevant stock exchange in the usual way. The choice of stock exchange impacts the style and content of the due diligence review. For example, a US -listed company needs to comply with specific U.S. Securities and

Exchange Commission (SEC) requirements including the Sarbanes-Oxley Act. This requires additional preparation and auditing of the company. The key output for an IPO due diligence is usually a prospectus, and accompanying documents such as long-form and short-form reports, which are used to sell the shares. These are highly structured and the specific information depends on the specific stock exchange where the listing is to take place.

For all markets, it is likely that the company has greater compliance requirements, and has to publish more financial and other commercial information openly.

How do you do a due diligence review?

The objectives for a due diligence review can be stated as:

- Obtain all the confirmed data and information required to assess the financial, legal & regulatory, and commercial information required to make decisions about the deal.
- Provide an insight into the target's business proposition including strategy, products, customer base, supply chain, operations, culture & style, people, tools and processes.
- Be able to form an opinion on whether and how the deal should proceed, by identifying any deal stoppers and confirming the right price to be paid (as per the initial offer 'heads of terms'). This is based on the business and the buyer's own medium to long-term objectives.

- Provide a basis for planning of the post-deal integration of people, processes and tools.

There are many approaches and tools for conducting due diligence assignments to achieve these objectives. Many organisations, especially the large accounting or legal firms, have also developed their own. For the purpose of this book we will follow the cycle:

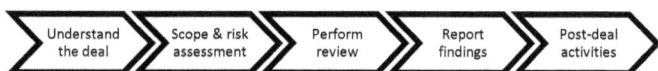

Each step is described next.

Step 1 Understand the business and the deal

Like all tight deadline/budget-restricted projects a due diligence exercise needs to be well planned and co-ordinated. Before planning can commence we need to obtain a high-level understanding of the business to identify potential risks and all benefits of the deal, including any not apparent from the information provided. This is sometimes referred to as the 'preparation step'. We have known deals be stopped at this stage because the information required for a full due diligence exercise was not available, or it became apparent that the deal was not in the strategic business interests of the buyer. The potential buyer concluded that if the target could not provide such high-level information, they were not in full control of their business and so there was a very high inherent risk.

The nature of the due diligence depends on whether we are working for the seller or the buyer. If we assume the buyer, there are two main models that may apply:

1. The buyer wishes to amalgamate the business into its own businesses to achieve some business benefits and synergies. These models are sometimes referred to as 'the Borg' as the business may be fully assimilated and lose its own identity (although sometimes brands may be kept for marketing advantage).

2. The business is kept as a separate entity with the view to selling it, or seeking stock market listing, in the medium to long term. This model fits with branded venture capital organisations such as the Virgin group, or private equity houses/venture capital trusts.

The nature of the purchaser's intentions is important as it drives the post-merger activity and also determines the style of due diligence review followed. This may depend on the objectives for the merger.

Horizontal mergers are where the merger is to achieve a larger market share. The target company is likely to have similar product or service offerings to those of the acquiring company (e.g. both in the food manufacturing industry) so the merger increases the proportion of the market taken by the new company. In some cases there may be anti-monopolistic/trust issues if the combined market share is seen as excessive compared to other competitors.

Alternatively the aim may be to add complementary processes of services to the acquiring organisation. In this case the strategic value of the offering may be the primary concern rather than the other review findings. Vertical mergers are where the aim is to improve control over the end to end process of the business rather than market share. This is the combining of entities in the same business sector, but a different level. For example, the target company may be a former supplier of the business, such as a component supplier for a motor manufacturer.

During the preparation stage we:

- obtain an overview of the deal and review, by:
  - o receiving a briefing from the client and advisors
  - o understanding the objectives of the deal, from both buyer and seller perspectives and the nature of the target
  - o assessing the high-level financial and legal information.
- agree confidentiality requirements – Given the sensitive nature of a due diligence assignment, and the highly confidential material that is required, formal confidentiality agreements are required. These may include the use of physical or web-based data rooms and the processes to be followed when accessing data. They may also include communications plans to ensure consistency of reporting to the buyer and/or seller, by whom and when, to ensure incomplete or inaccurate information is not supplied.
- form and prepare the review team – The team may consist of skilled project management & administration, financial, business, legal and IT professionals. Other specialists may be required depending on the deal (e.g.

people with knowledge and experience in post-deal integration, the relevant markets, banking and finance specialists). The team should have specific M&A experience. The responsibilities, including adherence to the rule of the engagement and adherence to reporting timelines, need to be fully understood by the team members. The team could be a mix of buyer staff and external professional advisors.

- identify areas for review and information requirements. This is key to ensuring all members of the review team are clear on their role and expected deliverables. This is recorded in the form of due diligence plans, checklists and data requests. These include the strategy and history of the target, management structures, financial and accounting results, assets, leases and so on and future performance forecasts.

In an ideal world IT specialists should be included at this stage to ensure all relevant IT issues have been identified and considered. We have found this where the client has critical IT applications, or is based in the IT/software sector, but often IT is overlooked until later in the review. This can make it difficult to obtain the information required in the remaining time available. Data validity and reliability feeds into the financial due diligence and so early warning of any issues could impact the whole of the review and its conclusions.

Step 2 Scope and risk assessment

The preparation stage should also include scoping and risk assessment. The risk assessment includes both the deal and the review.

Critical risk factors for the review may include:

- accessibility of staff at the target (especially given any labour relation issues regarding the future of the entity).
- accessibility and reliability of information provided.
- co-operation and team working of the review team.
- timelines and other constraints.
- external factors impacting the review (we have had to contend with religious holidays, picket lines and hurricanes!).
- failure to comply with confidentiality agreements, contractual obligations or specific regulatory requirements.

These factors apply equally to IT as to other areas of the business.

Critical success factors for the deal may include:

- financial viability and health.
- cultural fit.
- failure to provide adequate warranties or indemnities.
- future market position.
- excessive financial or other liabilities post-deal.

IT is an important factor in all the preceding factors.

Step 3 Perform review

The main purpose of the perform review stage is to gather and assess data. These are skills most IRM specialists are familiar with from other audits and reviews. We look to confirm the representations made by the target, validate their valuations and assessments, and scrutinise any legal, regulatory or compliance concerns. For example, the IT specialist may wish to look at Intellectual Property (IP) rights, data integrity and project planning. Often the buyer is also interested in softer issues, such as the professional capability of staff who may be acquired with the business and the culture and morale of the organisations, to assess how compatible they are with their own business. This may include the health of the relationship between IT and the rest of the organisation.

To assess whether the deal should proceed, and whether there needs to be negotiation over price, terms and conditions or deal shaping, the following questions may be addressed during the review:

- Are the accounting statements a comprehensive and 'true and fair' view of the current and likely future financial health of the target?

- Are financial forecasts accurate and realistic? (The review team may want to develop their own financial models for comparison.)

- How will the deal impact the profitability of the target business or the buyer?

- What is the commercial and business outlook, based on markets, competitor activity and the ability to increase earnings or reduce costs?

- Are there any exposures to wider financial (e.g. tax or pension liabilities) regulatory or liability risks (e.g. environmental concerns, legal changes impacting product offerings, recall risk on products)?

- Is the business sustainable in the medium to longer term? For example, this severely impacted the sale of chains of DVD rental and record companies after the increase in use of digital media.

- Are the company's management team of a high quality and capable of undertaking the changes required? (Some consider this to be *the* most important issue.)

- Are there any key staff who must be retained to ensure the future value creation or successful completion of the integration? This may include IT project and operation personnel.

- Are there any factors that could impact successful integration, e.g. culture clashes, overseas operational, environmental issues, labour disputes or other reputational issues?

Additional information may be required to complete the preceding. Specialists, such as IT, need to be aware of the full implications and impact of their findings and ensure review managers are kept informed of progress and potential findings. Really significant issues may also come to light that impact the review and deal – these need to be quickly discussed and resolved before proceeding. There are often daily or other regular meetings to ensure these issues are identified and assessed rather than being nasty surprises at the end of a long and expensive review.

Step 4 Report findings

The nature of the report depends on the assignment. For example, for an in-house M&A team review the report is likely to be relatively informal, in the form of a presentation of key facts. Where the review is conducted by an external firm the report is more structured (and longer) and may follow a prescribed format (e.g. for an IPO). The report needs to have clear conclusions and recommendations and provide sufficient evidence to support them. These recommendations may include a revised price or specific warranties and indemnities that are required.

Step 5 Post-deal

All too often post-deal integration is neglected. Without proper emphasis the synergies and business benefits identified are not achieved. Post-deal there may be significant integration activity, and the information gained during the review assists with this.

Debrief is also an important factor – what would be done differently for the next review. This could include earlier involvement of key specialists such as IT.

What could possibly go wrong?

Most reviews are conducted satisfactorily and reach a decision. Like most projects there can be periods of intense working and doubt, but these are usually overcome and a decision reached as to whether the deal should go ahead or not, or more often, under what terms and conditions it should proceed. Failure could result in missing an opportunity others see, or going ahead with a bad deal.

Common reasons for failure are that investigators:

- do not have open and full access to vital information.
- miss significant risks (including hidden opportunities) likely to significantly impact the deal.
- only consider their own area rather than the wider implications of their findings.
- ignore cultural issues.
- inadvertently disclose sensitive information.
- make emotional rather than logical and rational conclusions about the deal.

Most of these can be avoided by careful planning and scoping. Where there are significant assumptions, or lack of key information, this should be made very clear in the final report; this can be as revealing to the reader as stated facts and evidence provided. The stakeholders for a due diligence review place a great deal of reliance on the outcome. Contracts for due diligence work include clauses and other vehicles to reduce the risk on the reviewer. However, where a deal fails the affected parties may try to sue the advisors as an alternative to bringing a case against the seller. For example:

> When Hewlett-Packard Co. shareholders sued the company directors over the poor acquisition of Autonomy Corp., the company's auditors were also included as defendants. This case was subsequently dropped.

Summary and key take-aways

One analogy for due diligence is engagement and getting married. The due diligence phase is like an engagement: it shows a level of commitment between the parties, and a time for planning and discovery. Marriage is a binding commitment and involves trust – like business mergers it can be difficult (and some say expensive) to go back after the event. A broken engagement is better than a broken marriage and so walking away from a potentially bad deal following due diligence is better than finding out the consequences later. Having said that, due diligence should not be seen as a simple 'Go/No go' decision – more often it is 'Go but '. Both parties have a commitment to making the deal happen and so work to find ways to achieve this – perhaps through financial considerations (e.g. change to price), legal (e.g. contractual clauses) or commercial (e.g. agreements to work together jointly post-deal), or even in the case of marriage a pre-nuptial agreement. Just like marriage, in a good deal the benefits often outweigh the risks!

A due diligence assignment if run properly ensures the parties:

- are clear about what is being bought – reducing risk that valuations are ineffective or inaccurate, based on wrong assumptions.

- have asked deep enough questions – investigators need the tenacity to delve into difficult areas and not just accept the first answers they are given, or accepting blocks (rare as generally it's in the interviewee's interest to ensure review is successful).

- know the deal breakers or changes required to make the deal viable – the deal is only viable up to a certain price.

- have considered the cultural and 'fit' issues.

- are ready to begin integration based on findings.

- are not obsessed with completing the deal and ignoring warning signs. The analogy we often use here is falling in love with a quaint cottage property and ignoring the fact that the walls are subsiding.

We will see in the following chapters that IT professionals can have a key role to play in the successful completion of due diligence assignments.

CHAPTER 2: WHY IS IT IMPORTANT IN DUE DILIGENCE?

Overview

On many deals the value proposition may be underpinned by IT systems or data (e.g. future growth needs to be supported by more system or project investment, projects to deliver cost-savings/new capabilities, etc.). In addition the cost/investment assumptions around IT may not be realistic – exposing the purchaser to unforeseen costs and inadequate benefits from projects. When acquiring new businesses buyers often do not consider the IT systems and services for the company they are buying. Even large companies can have problems – for example, in 2012 computer issues impacted the ability of United Airlines to take reservations and to service customers following their merger with Continental.

IT can be the skeleton in the closet – where an information or data asset turns into a liability costing more than anticipated. Hidden costs can include licensing, maintenance, ongoing projects and support, incompatible systems or uncooperative staff/outsource providers. Although, other than for technology companies, IT considerations are rarely deal stoppers, they should be an important part of the negotiations, affecting the actual price paid or the shape of the final deal.

Information is a key business asset and can be central to many deals – high-quality reliable information is also required to help analyse financials, customer base and other key business indicators used during the actual due diligence review. In this chapter we look at some case studies of where IT issues can impact a transaction and how these can be overcome. In the following chapters we then consider how to apply some IT risk management tools and techniques so that each of these areas can be assessed in a due diligence review.

Case studies

The following case studies illustrate some of the ways that IT can play a positive part in due diligence exercises. Because of the confidential nature of due diligence, some of the details have been changed to protect the innocent (and not so innocent). We have also combined information from different reviews to form a single case study. The key elements of the cases are, however, realistic and represent issues that an IT specialist may be asked to address on due diligence reviews.

Case study 1: Buying an IT software company in 1999

This relates to a software company sale / acquisition in early 1999. At that time there were real concerns about 'Y2K' and potential liability. Although Y2K was a one-off occurrence, there may often be situations where the buyer needs reassurance about the quality of the technology they are buying.

The buyer was concerned that they could inherit a large liability if the software was found non-compliant for year 2000 date issues. This could have resulted in expensive lawsuits and costly changes required to the programme code, as well as potential reputational risks.

The buyer was keen on the purchase as it enhanced their product offering by offering a high-quality system for sale to their own customers. The seller was seeking to divest the company so that they could focus on other core business areas. The IT advisors' task was to assure the software was sound and would not be impacted by Y2K, or to find other ways that the deal could proceed with minimal risk.

Working as a team with lawyers and financiers for both parties, IT advisors had to provide technical input to review the quality of the programme code and the steps that had been taken to identify and resolve the risks associated with the Y2K issue. This resulted in warranties and other assurances being included in the contract, focusing on the higher-risk areas of the software code.

The deal went ahead, including suitable warranties and assurances. Although subsequently the Y2K issue was found to be nowhere near as big an issue as was thought, there was a real concern before the event. This could have stopped the deal, which was of strategic importance to the buyer and seller. No Y2K issues arose for the software and so there was no actual liability.

In the preceding the key elements were the validity of the software and the development process. It also illustrates that IT can have a wider impact on a deal, both in terms of its viability and the price and shape of the sale. In these situations IT advisors need to work as part of a multi-disciplinary team. Extra caution is required where meetings are attended by both buyer and seller. We have known situations where a few words spoken casually during a meeting were misinterpreted and nearly ended the whole deal. This is where previous experience of working on due diligence reviews is beneficial.

Case study 2: A confectioner whose systems were not so sweet

The owners of a manufacturer of confectionery products were considering selling the business and had asked for a pre-sale due diligence review. The company was a family concern that had grown through sales and the founders now wanted to sell to release capital so that they could travel the world as a family. There had been a modernisation programme to prepare the company for sale and this included the implementation of an Enterprise Resource Planning (ERP) system to manage the whole process through sales, production, inventory management and accounting. This system was to replace an aging accounting system, but the IT manager had little experience of a project of this type.

IT advisors were asked to undertake a review of the ERP project, the functionality to be delivered and the project's progress and likelihood of success. They were also asked to informally advise on the IT manager's competence.

By reviewing project plans, budgets and progress it became apparent that the project was running late and heavily over budget. There had been no clear definition of requirements and it was unlikely that the chosen solution as designed would meet key stakeholders' expectations. The review concluded that the project should be abandoned, reconsidered and started again in a more modest form.

The IT manager was replaced by someone with more project management and large-system experience. The sale was put on hold, the issues found for IT were similar throughout the organisation and so a new management team was brought in. They concentrated on implementing a smaller finance system that could later be extended to include other processes. This would give them the experience they needed in such implementations. The company was ready for sale within two years; a higher price was achieved, with the new management taking a stake. The previous owners literally sailed off into the sunset and enjoyed their well-earned retirement. The IT manager also got to spend more time with his family!

These forms of pre-due diligence review enable the seller to prepare the company for sale and get the best price possible. In this case there was a close emotional attachment – it was like someone selling the family home. The owners were proud of what they had achieved and found the separation difficult. Just like selling a house they needed to have a good spring clean and this included abandoning some projects, and indeed managers. To complete the review the due diligence team needed input from IT specialists with experience and knowledge of the selected ERP solution and project management.

Case study 3: Cheap as chips

Two years before this review a food manufacturer had acquired a business that included a chain of restaurants. They had fully integrated the business but had now decided to focus on core food manufacturing activities and so wished to sell the restaurants. The systems used were all standard packages, and had good reputations. They were also used to drive the business providing valuable management information for forecasting the growth of the business, seasonal sales, demand planning and so on. This included information provided to the potential buyer's (a venture capital company) IT advisors for the due diligence.

The IT advisors were asked to perform an initial high-level review of IT for the business focusing on people, tools and processes and to indicate areas where further work may be required. There was a need for discretion as the deal was highly confidential.

Under the guise of a regular audit the IT advisors performed a high-level review. Generally they found that the IT was fit for purpose, well established and respected in the business. However, three specific areas of concern were identified:

1. Data security for the customer loyalty scheme appeared to be poor – data servicing had been outsourced to a specialist provider and there was concern over the design and operation of data security controls. The IT advisors advised that a security review was conducted at the service provider. Controls were then found to be adequate.

2. The due diligence financial model used for forecasting was based on a spreadsheet and it was not clear how reliable this was. The IT advisors advised that an integrity and accuracy check was conducted on the spreadsheet model. No errors were found.

3. Much of the data processing for back-office systems belonged to the owner organisation and so the new company systems could not be segregated. A number of the key IT staff also worked for the parent company and would not be transferring as part of the sale. The IT advisors advised a review should be made of potential interim arrangements and the costs to replace systems in the medium term.

The deal went ahead following extensive negotiations. The final agreement included:

- specified key IT staff transferring to the new company.
- an adjustment in price to take account of the cost of implementing new systems.
- an interim service level agreement to allow the continued processing of systems for six months (with additional security controls).

This illustrates that IT advisors are not only auditors but also can make a positive contribution to the outcome of the deal. This required long hours (one person worked 105 hours in one week!) but the outcome was a good one for all concerned.

Case study 4: DIY software not an option

A chain of specialist shops was being sold. The previous IT manager had developed the main point of sales system in a long-forgotten coding language. This system was a frontline system and crucial to the success of the business. It also generated data used to provide sales forecasts for the deal. The former IT manager had retired and lived in a forest in Sweden – he could be (and was) contacted by sending messages to a post-office box. He was the only person able to maintain the system and did resolve issues but it could take a long time to get a response.

IT advisors for a potential buyer had been asked to review the IT of the operation. This included considering whether the point of sale system was fit for purpose and assessing the risks for future management and maintenance of the system.

A detailed review was conducted by an IT advisor with specific knowledge of these types of system. She found the code difficult to understand and there was little or no documentation. In addition some of the input screens had been designed to look like a commercially available software package (including the same spelling mistakes!). The advisors concluded that the system was not maintainable in its current form and would have to be replaced – this represented a major cost compared to the value of the business (it had been losing money for the last three years). Also there was a risk of litigation for plagiarism from the commercial software provider.

> The deal did not go ahead. It is believed that the
> software supplier brought a lawsuit. The company
> went into liquidation two years later.

The preceding illustrates that sometimes it's better to walk
away from a deal. Although IT was not the only issue for
this company, it illustrated their management style and
failure to control their business adequately.

Summary of IT considerations in due diligence

As we have seen in the preceding case studies, every due
diligence assignment is different. The significance of IT also
varies, but the main considerations are systems, data, projects
and IT service provision. The main IT considerations to
include in an IT or information due diligence are:

IT Consideration	Planning questions to ask
General	What IT audits have been conducted and how reliable are their findings?
	Does the target have any certifications or use any standard approaches for IT governance (e.g. PRINCE2®, ISO27001, COBIT®5 etc.).
Systems (see *Chapter 3*)	How reliant is the business on its IT infrastructure?
	What is being transferred? Is it transferable?

IT Consideration	Planning questions to ask
	Is IT well maintained and current? Is documentation available and reasonable?
	Are there adequate controls to protect the confidentiality/integrity and availability of information systems and data?
IT Security (see *Chapter 4*)	Have there been any security breaches?
	Would a breach have serious consequences for the due diligence review or ongoing business post-merger?
	Does the target have an IT security policy and are there indications that it is applied?
Data (see *Chapter 5*)	Is data clean and of good quality?
	Is it of value?
	Would incomplete or inaccurate data have serious consequences for the due diligence review or ongoing business post-merger?
Projects and Change (see *Chapter 6*)	Are current projects likely to complete on time and budget?
	Would failure to complete these projects have serious consequences for the due diligence review or ongoing business post-merger?
IT Service	Will it be possible to easily separate

IT Consideration	Planning questions to ask
Provision (see *Chapter 7*)	the IT from the parent company or will alternative arrangements be required?
	Does the IT staff have the right skills, experience and qualifications?
	Are they at the right price for their skills?
	Are savings possible or are there signs of underinvestment?
	Will they fit the new culture or will differences impact current projects or IT service delivery?

CHAPTER 3: SYSTEMS REVIEWS

Overview

We now understand what IT due diligence is and why it is important. Here we discuss how we actually plan and undertake these reviews. Our initial focus is on reviewing systems. Systems are defined as the IT infrastructure, hardware, middleware and software required to support the key business processes. We should remember that IT is an enabler; it is not a business process in its own right but facilitates such processes. Consequently it is very rare that IT due diligence is carried out independently of financial due diligence, so we should plan to work as an integrated team. It is likely that the business being acquired or sold has already worked with the financial due diligence team to identify the key business processes. Hence it is our role to perform a risk analysis to identify the key systems that underpin these business processes. We are not interested in all the systems, only the key ones, i.e. those relevant to the deal and future business plans.

The main purpose of the systems review is to see whether the systems are fit for purpose for the new organisation and will help it achieve the business plans and have the benefits desired from the deal. The following chart identifies the process to conduct such a systems review:

Risk analysis ▷ Identify key systems ▷ Reliability ▷ Upgrade & patching strategy ▷ Regulatory requirements ▷ Business requirements

IT security and data security are both part of systems reviews; however, because of the importance of the security of IT and data they are covered separately in later chapters.

Risk analysis

As a *component* of *risk management*, risk analysis consists of:

- identification of possible negative external and internal *conditions*, *events*, or situations.
- determination of cause-and-effect (causal) relationships between probable happenings, their *magnitude* and likely outcomes.
- e*valuation* of various outcomes under different *assumptions*, and under different *probabilities* that each outcome will take place.
- application of *qualitative* and *quantitative techniques* to reduce *uncertainty* of the outcomes and *associated costs, liabilities or losses*.

The purpose of the risk analysis is to identify and categorise the entity-level risks the organisation is managing. This is a joint phase with the financial due diligence team.

Case study

A European airline identified one of the entity-level risks as refunds. If the passenger did not travel, they had up to five years to claim a refund on a full fare for this full service carrier. It decided not to fully provide for the liability of tickets not used to travel.

Identify key systems

The organisation may have documented the key business processes. It is important that this document is accurate, complete and up-to-date otherwise we work with the management team and the financial due diligence team to identify these key business processes. For most organisations the key processes and the systems they interact with are easily identifiable. At a high level they are those processes that create value, revenue streams, control costs and manage cash flow.

When working with the financial due diligence team and the management team, there are two main methods of identifying the key processes and systems. These are the financial value of transactions and the volume of transactions processed by each system, as illustrated in the following diagram:

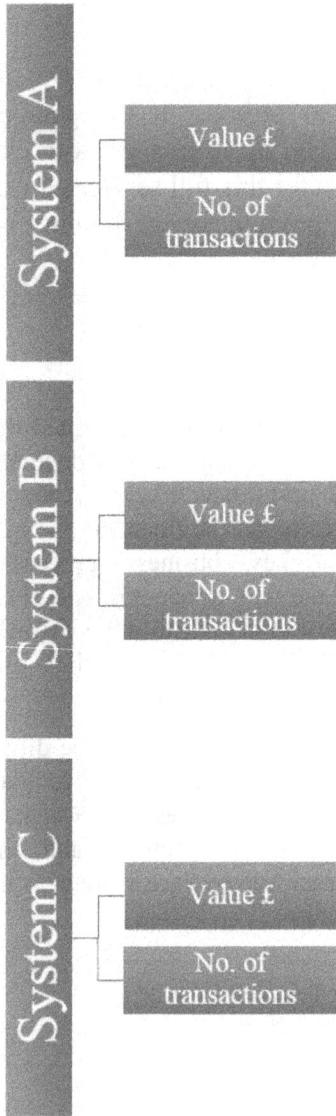

In respect of agreeing what constitutes high enough financial values we agree what is termed a materiality level with the financial due diligence team and management. In the preceding example systems A and B could be included in the scope, and the value and/or number of transactions processed excludes system C from the scope.

An alternative method is identifying the key business processes by looking at the monetary value and number of transactions processed and the supporting systems.

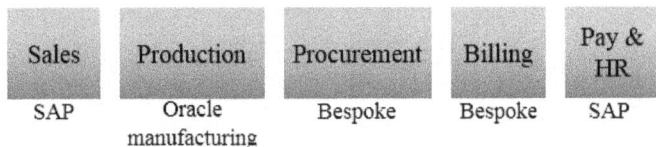

Sales	Production	Procurement	Billing	Pay & HR
SAP	Oracle manufacturing	Bespoke	Bespoke	SAP

In the preceding example we agree with the financial due diligence team and management that SAP, Oracle and the bespoke procurement and billing applications are material and in scope due to the value and/or the number of transactions being processed, but the outsourced payroll and HR application is not.

We could also look at the reliability and maturity of systems, staff familiarity and workarounds to inform our decision.

However, it is the actual operation of those systems and whether any documentation is up to date that is the real question. It is not unusual for us to be the first people to document the key processes!

> **Case study**
>
> A loan company was the target of a takeover. At the time of the acquisition approach the company was updating its loan application process from paper-based to an online portal. The success of this development was pivotal to the value of the company. We worked with management to walk through each stage of the process to understand how the new portal would interact with existing back-office systems.

Once we understand the key processes we walk through and document each process and seek to understand their interaction with the wider systems.

Reliability of the key systems

The business requirement for systems reliability or availability depends on the industry. An online bank requires systems to be up 100% of the time. An office service company can operate for several days without its systems.

We look at the following to help us assess the value an organisation places on each key system's resilience and reliability:

- IT strategy.
- The age of the applications and supporting infrastructure.
- Whether the systems are still supported by the suppliers.

- Maintenance strategy and unplanned downtime of the systems due to incidents and problems.
- System resilience strategy.
- IT security.

Some organisations view their IT systems as integral to their success and keep them up to date whether they are ERP systems, i.e. organisation wide, or a mixture of what are known as best of breed systems and are usually process specific, e.g. sales systems. Best of breed may be package systems or in-house developed bespoke systems. Whether or not the system is a package solution or in-house developed we cover the same aspects when looking at reliability.

Businesses change over time, as do their processes. To fully support the business the systems need to evolve and change in line with the business to ensure they continue to meet the business requirements. If the systems do not change to meet the current way the business operates, we invariably end up with the nightmare of 'workarounds' and a myriad of spreadsheets supporting the core systems. Spreadsheets are rarely developed rigorously and contain mistakes and their designs are seldom covered by adequate documentation.

The starting point for assessing an organisation's attitude to the resilience and reliability of the systems is looking at the IT strategy to see what the organisation's appetite has been for updating the systems. If the systems are not updated regularly, it is likely they are old, unpatched and potentially subject to security vulnerabilities. It is not unusual to find systems that are at least ten tears old still in use. At best these old systems are inefficient. At worst they hide significant errors that have impact the financial statements.

> **Case study**
>
> A shipping company relied on spreadsheets to provide management information that the old core systems could not provide. During the due diligence process errors were identified in the spreadsheets exposing a $20m hole in the balance sheet. The shareholders received a significantly reduced price per share.

We look at the versions of the systems and supporting infrastructure. The organisation does not need to be on the latest versions. This could bring issues in terms of untested functionality or bugs! Being one or two versions behind the release curve is acceptable. Upgrading and patching is covered in more detail next.

Access to the help desk and their records is critical in this phase of the due diligence. The amount of unplanned downtime or systems failure and high-category incidents and problems is a good indicator of poor systems reliability and the possibility of data and records kept out of system.

Upgrade and patching strategy

Having identified the age of the systems, we see whether they are still supported by the suppliers in terms of upgrades and maintenance and security patches. Suppliers only provide support for older version for a period of time. Microsoft has withdrawn support for its XP operating system 12 years after its launch and 10 years after Windows Server 2003 was launched.

For package systems and operating systems having access to regular upgrades and patches gives access to the latest functionality and security features. New functionality is provided in upgrades typically, and patches are used to mitigate the risk of failure and security breaches. Organisations that keep up to date or up to date minus a version indicate a well thought out upgrade and patching strategy. Where such a strategy is used the risk of systems failure is usually lower.

Maintenance of bespoke systems is more difficult. A strategy has to be agreed to keep the system up to date to meet business requirements. We are not discussing the systems development lifecycle in this book but it is important to assess how the organisation is upgrading and patching bespoke systems. A good indicator of reliability is if it is like painting Sydney Harbour Bridge: a never-ending process with a dedicated team monitoring reliability and regular projects to upgrade to maintain functionality and security.

Systems resilience strategy

This is another area that depends on the industry that the target organisation is in. An airline requires its ticket sales, seat allocation, checking in and flight management systems to be available 24/7. We would expect the systems to be mirrored at an off-site location.

A property management company typically would not require such a high level of availability. As long as the systems are automatically backed up to an off-site location and a business continuity plan and disaster recovery plan detail the order in which systems need to be restored this is often sufficient.

We need to understand what is typical for the industry.

IT security

Up to the beginning of the 21st century it was sufficient to look at passwords and their complexity. With the massive growth in data caused by the global economy and systems being integrated across organisations, IT security is a subject that is itself complex and has a chapter to itself (*Chapter 4*).

Regulatory requirements

As a business develops, business practices mature and become sharper and the man in the street appears to be developing a growing mistrust of big business. This increases the pressures for additional regulation. Since the Enron scandal, the various banking frauds and of course the financial crash in 2008, industry regulation has grown to such an extent that it almost occupies its own sector in the economy.

Compliance with regulation cannot be overlooked when assessing business processes and systems, so our walkthrough not only considers integrity, efficiency, suitability and resilience but also identifies weaknesses that could mean non-compliance with regulation such as the Data Protection Act.

Case study

A defence company was forbidden by UK Government regulation from dealing with specific countries. In assessing the systems we looked at whether controls in the systems prevented doing business with those countries. The systems looked at included whether the email prevented communication. The systems were appropriately controlled and configured.

Summary and key take-aways

In conducting the system review we look at a variety of what might seem unconnected subjects. In actual fact they are an interconnected web. At the top level we see if the systems are fit for purpose by considering:

- the business and regulatory requirements and whether the systems facilitate or hinder the operation of the business and its compliance with regulations. We walk through the processes and the regulations to see how the systems meet those requirements.
- the age of the systems and the frequency of system failures.
- the upgrading and patching strategy and whether it is appropriate for the situation.
- systems resilience strategy and whether it is appropriate for the industry.
- the IT security measures and whether they are appropriate for the situation.

CHAPTER 4: IT SECURITY

Overview

IT security was rarely a separate topic in the scope of IT due diligence until five years ago and the high risk for intellectual property to be accessed and stolen by hackers. It deserves its own chapter because if intellectual property is being stolen, the value of the company reduces the longer it remains defenceless and the hack goes undetected. Due to the high risk of hacking in many sectors, IT security is now a boardroom topic and chief executive officers (CEOs) and chief financial officers (CFOs) have at least an appreciation of it. There have even been cases where sensitive information about M&A transactions has been allegedly hacked during due diligence reviews.

Many organisations strive to have their information security management system (ISMS) certified to ISO27001. We are not discussing how to achieve certification in this book but if you are looking to achieve certification then Alan Calder's *Nine Steps to Success: An ISO27001 (2013) Implementation Overview* is a no-nonsense guide for first-time implementers.

As with all IT systems, technology is not the only factor we have to consider. Our favourite three components are particularly relevant here: process, people and technology.

We suggest that how these three elements interact with the organisation is also critical in IT security. ISACA's Business Model for Information Security readily illustrates this.

Senior management of an organisation is responsible for the level of awareness and behaviour towards IT security and the governance of the security processes – known as the security culture. Technology enables and supports the security processes. People design and maintain those processes and other people are supposed to operate the systems in compliance with these processes – the human factor.

The IT security threat landscape is constantly changing and depending on the target (of due diligence) organisation can be subject to a global or international threat or, at least as important, a threat from within.

There are four main areas of IT security threat:

1. State-sponsored hacking
2. Organised crime
3. 'Hacktivist'
4. Internal to the organisation.

State-sponsored hacking is where certain countries acquire economic knowledge by hacking the systems, usually by a complex Trojan horse, and extracting information in a constant feedback to the offending state. McAfee has a well-documented case study, Night Dragon, of state-sponsored hacking of five oil and gas companies.

How is state-sponsored hacking relevant to a due diligence project? It is much the same as if the doors to the research and development or design offices were left wide open. People would come in and steal the designs, see how our products were made and copy them, thus gaining intimate knowledge of the company's intellectual property and its value would fall. State-sponsored hacking is exactly the same and opens the systems of the company to the theft of intellectual capital or knowledge. Such hacks can often go undetected for years if an effective ISMS is not implemented. If such a hack is discovered during due diligence, the value of the company significantly reduces.

Organised crime is the hacking of systems to gain from crime. Several banks have suffered from key logging devices being fitted onto computers to enable criminals to bypass security features in the systems and steal millions of dollars/pounds and so on. In another case drug smugglers hid drugs among legitimate cargo in shipping containers; they subcontracted the hacking of the port's systems to enable them to remove the containers before the legitimate customer arrived.

Hacking by organised crime is the same as leaving the safe door open and allowing all to steal the money from it. The prime objective is to make financial gain. Again, if funds can be stolen relatively easily, it indicates perimeter controls are weak. So it can have a detrimental effect on the value of the company.

'Hacktivists' are the activists who hack systems to cause reputational damage to defence companies, drugs companies, construction firms and other high-profile causes. Normally the attack is either defacing a website or conducting a distributed denial-of-service attack rather than direct economic damage.

Reputational damage to a company can devalue it as much as the loss of data or funds. If the wider community believes the 'hacktivist', the company can be devalued. Sony paid a high price when its PlayStation network was taken down for weeks and millions of user accounts were accessed by a group known as LulzSec. It is estimated to have cost the company $100m. However, it is well documented the highest risk for all organisations is the accidental hack caused by poor processes or the disgruntled employee deliberately damaging the systems.

Due diligence projects are interested in the internal control systems because if there are poor processes and weak controls, it can indicate that the environment is open to systemic errors. In performing IT due diligence we have to consider the threat landscape that the organisation is exposed to.

Assessing the ISMS

The following process summarises how we assess the ISMS.

Risk Assessment → IT Security Strategy → IT Security Policy → Perimeter Security → Internal Security → Response Plan

Risk assessment

We look at the industry and the type of IT security threat it faces. To an extent we use our knowledge and experience because there is no legal or regulatory requirement to report IT security breaches, although the forthcoming European Directive on Data Security will enforce a reporting regime if it is passed without further reform. We work with the chief information security officer (CISO) and data protection officer (DPO) to understand the threats the organisation faces.

An important point to consider is whether the organisation is devolved with little central direction and policy or centralised with an overall corporate policy and systems. The devolved scenario can introduce security risks for the organisation because it is easy to leave weaknesses in the perimeter where there is no central direction and strategy. This is like designing a maze. If there is one person designing it, there is one entry point and a specific route to the end. When a group of people design the maze without central direction there could be several entry points and routes to the end making it much easier to navigate. Where individual subsidiaries are responsible for the design, implementation and maintenance of security it is easy to leave potential entry points in the wider group network for the hacker to enter.

The location of the company and its offices and subsidiaries around the world, customer and supplier relationships and the supply chain should be comprehended so that the countries where business is conducted are understood. We now need to look at the laws and regulations for each of the countries. With the strongest laws assessed, the entire organisation needs to comply with the strongest regulations throughout the organisation, especially where data can be stored in the Cloud and/or overseas data centres where the regulations are likely to be relatively weak.

The data room is the starting point to review the current documentation provided by the CISO, internal and external audit reports and any certification audit reports, such as for ISO27001, that will contribute to the risk assessment.

IT security strategy

The IT security strategy informs us of the measures the organisation plans to implement or update.

We need to assess whether the IT security strategy is appropriate for the situation and, if implemented, will it maintain compliance with the corporate governance requirements local laws and regulations.

IT security policy

Reviewing the IT security policy informs us of what the internal users are allowed to do with the IT and how the risk of the user is mitigated.

An important area to look at is whether the users have to acknowledge they have read the IT policy. For this to be effective of course it has to be concise, easy to understand, effective and not be as long as *War and Peace*.

Perimeter security

If the risk assessment indicates a significant external threat, we assess the effectiveness of the perimeter security measures. Traditionally this would be firewalls but today they are no longer sufficient. However, let's start with the firewalls.

The firewall is a system that is designed to prevent unauthorised access from outside a network. It has rules that define what access is specifically allowed and what is not and then a drop-dead rule as a catch-all for all other undesirable traffic trying to access the systems. To be effective the rules need to be regularly maintained and not too complex because it is easy to implement rules that counteract existing rules.

Our scope, therefore, covers the strategy for maintaining the firewall rules.

Antivirus policy and strategy is also an important area to assess. Although antivirus measures can be negated by a hacker introducing a Trojan horse, for example, for normal operation the detection and removal of viruses needs to be done quickly and efficiently. Our assessment looks at whether the virus definitions are kept up to date (normally daily at a minimum) and whether all areas of the network and portable equipment are covered. In addition how is portable equipment kept up to date with the antivirus software and virus definitions?

Unfortunately the threat and technology today means these traditional methods are no longer sufficient to keep the network safe. Depending on what our risk assessment has indicated we may also need to look at traffic and network monitoring services and/or software, such as that offered by organisations such as Damballa Inc and FireEye Inc. These are designed to identify suspicious activity on the network and use this intelligence to uncover threats and help to design mitigating controls.

Internal security

As discussed earlier, for almost every organisation the accidental security breach and disgruntled employee is the biggest threat. Many organisations now use internally focused network monitoring to identify internal threats.

The traditional review of IT security is still valid here:

- Complex passwords but not so complex they have to be written down.
- No sharing of user credentials.
- Regular changing of passwords.
- Timely removal of leavers' access rights.
- Tailoring access rights to roles.

Penetration testing

Penetration testing is the ethical hacking of an organisation's network and systems to expose weaknesses in the security. It should look for both external and internal threats. High-profile organisations should have penetration testing conducted regularly and act upon the findings. If there has not been a recent test conducted, this could be part of the due diligence scope.

Response plan

Should the subject of our due diligence be unfortunate to suffer a security breach there should be a response plan. A Trojan horse can take a number of years to fully eliminate and the business still needs to operate while potentially still losing economically valuable data.

We ascertain whether the response plan is appropriate for the situation.

Physical security

This is less sexy than preventing hacking, but physical security and knowing where your data is actually located is equally important. We discuss data management and security in a later chapter.

Many major companies and organisations outsource the service provision of their IT and are dependent on the security controls operated by their service provider. Equally, if the organisation itself hosts its IT, the same physical security measures should be looked for:

- Staff display passes that include their access rights that show to which areas of the building they are permitted and which areas are 'off-limits'. Only those staff who maintain and monitor the systems in the data centre should be allowed access.

- The data centre should be dedicated to that purpose and, for example, a print room should be elsewhere.

- There should be dual power supply from separate sources feeding the data centre and then a final backup of an uninterruptible power supply system (UPS).

- A fire suppression system.

- Outsourced data centres can equally host the organisation's competitors systems as well. The service provider should provide dedicated cages for each client's servers.

- Cloud provision makes our life more challenging but the service provider still needs to identify where our systems are hosted so that, for example, our client is not breaking trade restrictions.

The most secure data centres we have seen are situated in obscure locations, invariably off-site and give no outward appearance of being a data centre. Access is strictly controlled by employing biometrics such as fingerprint or iris technology. The core of the data centre is surrounded by a firebreak corridor where under anything but the most extreme fire event people can survive while the fire is extinguished in the equipment room by inert chemical or synthetic gas.

Where the service provision of IT is outsourced it is important to ensure the service provider has been externally assessed to ensure their systems are secure, reliant and compliant with regulations and legislation. It is important to remember that you may be able to transfer the responsibility for data processing and storage but you can seldom transfer the risk of data loss. These service providers may also have an ISAE3000 or ISAE3402 report from an appropriate organisation on which we can rely for our due diligence. It is important to review any report to ensure the assessor has covered all elements that are important to you.

Summary and key take-aways

IT security, or probably more correctly technology security, is currently an ever-changing field as the threat landscape continues to change. Our scope is directed by the risk assessment and what threats the organisation faces.

By far the biggest threat for all organisations is the accidental security breach created by poor processes and the disgruntled employee threat. However, in today's global economy organisations may also face one or more threats from:

- State-sponsored hacking
- Organised crime hacking
- 'Hacktivist' hacking.

In performing our due diligence we need to ascertain whether the security measures in place are appropriate to mitigate the risk to the organisation.

CHAPTER 5: DATA REVIEWS

Overview

A survey by Symantec (the data security company) in 2012 found that respondents said that information/data represented about 49% of organisations' total value. However, the value of data and the costs of transforming, merging, storing and securing it are often excluded from a due diligence review. Also the value of the data to the new company may be different to that given to it by the existing company. There could be a synergy by merging the data, for example, within certain constraints, providing marketing access to new markets, or other information based on geographies. Consider, for example, a luxury goods company acquiring a new business with a similar customer profile but a different product.

Data is also used during the due diligence review itself and so some consideration needs to be given to the quality and reliability of data, particularly if used within models used as a basis for merger and acquisition decision making.

In this chapter we consider:

- considering data during due diligence preparation.
- reviewing data issues.
- data privacy considerations.

At the end of the chapter there is also a summary and key take-aways.

Considering data during due diligence preparation

During the preparation stage it is important to assess the significance of data for the review and the deal. The emphasis is likely on the financial costs and benefits of data, and the associated risks. There are a number of issues to consider:

Data costs and benefits

We need to understand the significance of data for this deal. This includes taking an inventory of the key data and assessing its quality. If the significance is low, we do not need to perform extensive work during the due diligence review. If it is significant, during the review we perform a full data audit to assess the quality of the data to be provided. Six key questions to consider during the preparation stage are:

1. What data does the target hold , e.g. to support sales, production, finance, HR and other back-office systems?

2. What information do management and directors use to monitor the company and how is this extracted from current systems? How do they ensure the integrity of this information?

3. What is the structure for data ownership, quality etc.? Is this supported by documentation?

4. Will data be merged with that of the acquiring organisation? If so, is it structured in a similar way?

5. What historic data will be transferred? Is it from a single data or multiple databases, and what are the volumes and quality?
6. Will data need to be archived, particularly of applications that are decommissioned or replaced?

The main issues are explored later in the "Performing a data audit" section.

Regulatory and compliance risks

The purchaser may not be aware of the risks associated with the confidentiality of data, particularly personal or sensitive customer data. Take airline ticket data, for example, which can hold information relating to religious beliefs (such as requesting a kosher or halal meal). The requirements vary for different countries. Compliance failure can be very expensive, in fines, other penalties and in loss of reputation. The following three questions during the preparation stage help to assess the significance of regulatory and compliance issues:

1. Are there any data privacy or protection issues to consider?
2. Are there any specific sector regulatory requirements for data (e.g. 'treating customers fairly' requirements in the finance sector)?
3. Are data retention and other policies compatible with the acquiring organisation's?

There is significant overlap with IT security (see *Chapter 4*). The specific data privacy considerations are discussed shortly under "Data privacy reviews".

Use of data during the due diligence review

By reviewing data used for the due diligence exercise we can provide the review team with assurance as to the assumptions they make about future growth of the business. In addition it provides us with an insight as to how easily data can be extracted from existing systems and an indication of its quality. Two questions to consider during the preparation stage are:

1. Will the target provide data for the due diligence review (e.g. historic sales information by division or data to support the financial forecasts for the valuation of the entity?

2. What steps will be taken to ensure the accuracy and completeness of the data provided, including any transformations or predictions modelled from that data?

The section "Reviewing the forecast and other due diligence models" section is applicable where these issues are relevant.

Reviewing data issues

Performing a data audit

The objectives of a data audit could be summarised as:

Review all the target's relevant key data, to consider the arrangements for its stewardship, and controls to ensure its quality and integrity and confidence in its use.

The main parts of this definition are:

1. Key data	Implies we identify and classify all data so that can focus on what is key to the business and the deal. For example, finance data is relevant to nearly all deals, whereas HR data may only be relevant for those businesses with a high labour input, e.g. recruitment agencies or other service-based companies.
2. Arrangements for its stewardship	This includes all arrangements for classifying and securing data: ensure clear ownership and arrangements for its collection, maintenance, archiving and final destruction. The transfer of ownership of data is as significant as any other asset as failure to transfer data could lead to additional expense, loss of income/customers and potential damage to the reputation or brand.
3. Controls to ensure its quality and integrity and confidence	This includes controls over data capture, whether data is sourced internally or externally, ensuring consistency between different data sources and reducing duplication or replication of data items in different systems. It

	also includes controls to ensure data is easily accessible, when required and authorised.

The deal itself or the circumstances surrounding it could also increase the risk of loss of data to competitors. The volumes of data that can be stored on small devices and simply put into someone's pocket are huge. One oil major suffered a security breach with contact details of 170,000 employees and contractors.

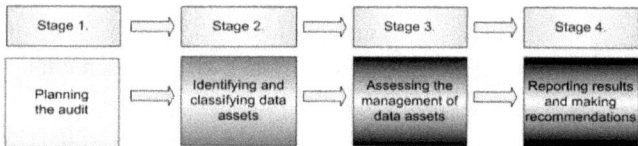

The four stages of the Data Audit Framework, per Jones Ross and Ruuselepp, University of Glasgow[1]

There are four main stages to the Data Audit Framework:

1. Planning the audit.
2. Identifying and classifying data assets.
3. Assessing the management of data assets.
4. Reporting findings and recommending change.

---

[1] *The Data Audit Framework by Jones Ross and Ruuselepp,* Humanities Advanced Technology and information Institute, (HATII), University of Glasgow (*www.data-audit.eu/DAF_Methodology.pdf*), Release: Version 1.8, May 2009.

Reviewing the forecast and other due diligence models

Significant reliance is placed on financial models for M&A due diligence. These may be spreadsheets or similar reports provided by the target, or models based on different assumptions using data provided. A number of surveys have concluded that most spreadsheets contain errors. A model commonly consists of:

- some form of revenue or income and expenditure statement.
- balance sheet.
- analysis of sales.
- analysis of assets.
- cash flow forecasts.
- tax and other cost predictions.

These can involve complex calculations and changing assumptions. Add in the time and other pressures during due diligence and there is a very high risk of error. The implication is that pricing and benefit evaluation calculations are incorrect, leading to bad decisions and the wrong price being paid for the acquisition. The solution is often that the merger and acquisition team request an audit of the spreadsheet and data to confirm its accuracy and reliability. A number of independent firms offer this service and a range of tools (including in-built into MS Excel) can be used. Reviews often include assessing guidelines and processes for modelling, integrity checks on data, checking every cell, an analytical review of results and the recalculation of key values.

Given the risk of this type of review the liability of the auditor is often restricted to a ratio of the fee or some other monetary limit. Hence there is still an emphasis on the requestor of the service to ensure the models are accurate. The review can only reduce the risk of errors in the model – it can never fully eliminate it. This risk can be reduced if a review is properly scoped and uses a solid approach, aiming to identify significant errors or omissions.

Some of the common errors made are:

- mixing input data, calculations and results on the same sheets. Good models spate these so that data can be easily changed as assumptions about the deal change. This also allows for automated entry of data.

- including embedded assumptions in cells (e.g. entering a VAT rate as 17.5%, rather than using a variable that can be changed for different tax areas), or having inconsistent calculations in cells in a single column (e.g. totals across then one entry that is derived in a different way).

- errors in referencing data or other sheets.

- failure to use control totals to check the validity of data received. Cross-referencing and checking totals is a good control to ensure consistency across sheets.

- lack of version or change controls or restriction to access (e.g. by locking cells containing calculations).

- reliance on a single modeller rather than having a peer review.

Given the significance of models good security measures would also be expected.

Data privacy considerations

Data privacy covers the handling of personal, especially sensitive data. There are a number of different laws and requirements around the world, some with very significant penalties including large fines, imprisonment and withdrawal of data processing facilities/data destruction. Although the details of different legislation vary, the basic principles are the same. The UK requirements are that personal data shall:

- be processed fairly and lawfully and, in particular, shall not be processed unless certain stated conditions are met.

- be obtained only for one or more specified and lawful purposes, and shall not be further processed in any manner incompatible with that purpose or those purposes.

- be adequate, relevant and not excessive in relation to the purpose or purposes for which they are processed.

- be accurate and, where necessary, kept up to date.

- only be processed for any purpose or purposes and shall not be kept for longer than is necessary for that purpose or those purposes.

- be processed in accordance with the rights of data subjects under this Act.

- be protected by appropriate technical and organisational controls. Measures shall be taken against unauthorised or unlawful processing of personal data and against accidental loss or destruction of, or damage to, personal data.

- not be transferred to a country or territory outside the European Economic Area unless that country or territory ensures an adequate level of protection for the rights and freedoms of data subjects in relation to the processing of personal data.

Very similar principles apply throughout Europe and other areas have also adopted similar principles. Underlying these principles are requirements to allow the data subject access to review and request amendment to erroneous data. The likely impact of data privacy for a merger or acquisition depends on the nature of the deal and the resulting organisation. If, for example, the organisation has very little personal data, or will not introduce any new countries after the merger, the impact is likely to be very low.

The IT specialist on the due diligence review should be aware of the data privacy requirements and perform an impact assessment to assess the extent to which data privacy needs to be considered. This could include use of data during the due diligence review, especially with the increasing use of e-data rooms, whereby deal information can be reviewed via secure links from virtually anywhere in the world. When performing a data privacy impact assessment, consideration needs to be given to:

- identifying all countries/legal domains where data is collected, transferred, stored or processed and understanding the data privacy requirements of each (there are special considerations where data is transferred to the US, for example).

- whether the deal will change the way that the data will be shared or used, especially where this is different to that explained to data subjects at the time of collection.
- continuing to use data fairly and in accordance with requirements.
- assessing what personal data is held and the stated purposes when it was originally obtained.

One outcome may be that data cannot be transferred, or that all data subjects need to be communicated with to be given the right to have their data removed or amended. If, for example, data subjects have opted out of marketing, these must still be honoured after a merger. This can be particularly difficult where systems or databases are being merged.

The balance between personal data privacy and the need for state or other security access is seen differently in different countries and this is likely to be a big issue in data privacy over the next few years.

Summary and key take-aways

The consideration of data issues could be significant for some deals. Consideration needs to be given to the data held and also specific requirements for data privacy.

CHAPTER 6: REVIEWING PROJECTS AND CHANGES IN PROGRESS

Overview

Change programmes and projects are frequently a business as usual activity for many organisations with projects on the go all the time and naturally have an impact on due diligence exercises.

Failed IT projects cost the world's largest 500 companies more than $14billion per year says the National Association of Corporate Directors in the US.

We need to ascertain which projects are material to the due diligence exercise. To a certain extent we need to cross-refer to the systems review (see *Chapter 3*). If a project impacts any of the key systems or processes then this project must be included in the list of projects to be reviewed during due diligence.

Projects often incur significant costs so the size of the investment also contributes to the selection of the project for review in the due diligence exercise. Smaller investments can have a major impact on business-critical systems and processes, e.g. IT security. Although regulatory projects often involve large investments they should always be included in the due diligence scope.

The following chart is a decision tree for whether a project/programme should be included in the due diligence scope.

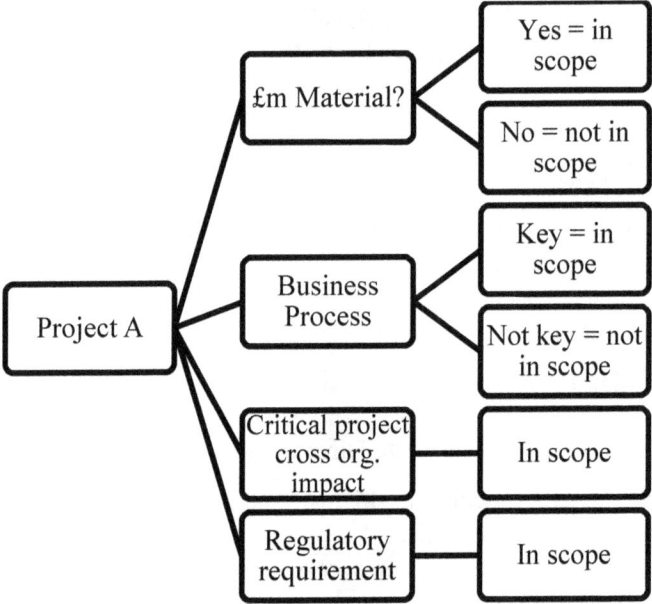

Auditors are very familiar with reviewing projects using the traditional waterfall project management methodologies such as PRINCE2; however, project implementation methodologies are developing and Agile is now becoming common due to the flexibility it offers. We are not looking at methodologies in detail in this chapter but if this is the first time you are seeing an Agile project, Chris Wright's book *Agile Governance and Audit: An overview for auditors and agile teams* is an excellent guide.

The rest of this chapter discusses how we carry out a project review, irrespective of the project methodology.

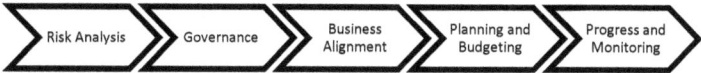

Risk analysis

The objective of the risk analysis is to assess the impact of the project on the organisation in terms of:

- Is the project going to deliver something that will benefit the new organisation post-deal?
- Is the project providing value for money? Or is the budget too restrictive?
- What will the impact on the organisation be if the project does not deliver or delivers less than planned?
- What will the impact on the organisation be if what is delivered does not work?

It is well documented that IT projects fail to deliver what was planned on a regular basis. Do a Google search and you can find the failure rate is somewhere between 50% and 75%.

If we were betting men, we would say it is almost a dead cert that the organisation has at least one major project underway during our due diligence! The project will have been planned at some point in the past, probably a long time before a deal was thought of.

We see if the project is going to deliver a system the post-deal organisation can benefit from. Our assessment looks at what is delivered and whether it fits with the post-deal strategy for the new organisation, e.g.:

- Is the platform in common with what is intended to be used?
- Is the software in common with what is intended to be used?
- Is the functionality in line with future business requirements?
- Can it easily be scaled for the larger organisation?
- Will the project team be transferred over to the new organisation or will they be redundant in the new organisation?

Governance

We assess the chances of success of the project. Governance has a key role to play in the success of projects.

Here we look at sponsorship of the project and whether the sponsor is of an appropriate level of senior management. The expectation is that for major projects sponsorship should be at 'C' level.

As well as the level of sponsor we look to see that they are active in the project, receiving progress reports, risk registers, issues lists and key change requests and are dealing with these appropriately. The sponsor should be making decisions where necessary and providing guidance on scope and challenging where appropriate. A judgement call is required on the:

- competence of the sponsor.

- the involvement of the sponsor.

In addition to looking at the sponsorship of the project we need to assess whether the sponsor is appropriately supported by the project management and the business through bodies such as the steering committee.

What we are looking for is that the committee structure is used to assist the project and help to resolve dispute.

Business alignment

The business case and requirements are key and as suggested previously the detail depends on the project methodology used. However, we should be able to ascertain whether the business requirements have been considered and if the project is aligned with the business strategy.

Business benefits should also be defined in measurable terms, e.g.:

- Significant cost savings per annum.
- The workforce will be reduced by 'X' full-time equivalents.
- Revenue leakage will be reduced by 'X' per annum.

Planning and budgeting

The project management is assessed to see if the project is well planned and appropriate for the methodology used. A project plan should be monitored and regularly updated to facilitate the on-time delivery of the project.

Projects where the plan is not updated and monitored is highly likely not to deliver what is intended.

Similarly, the budget also needs updating and monitored against actual cost through the project lifecycle.

Change management

All projects need to change the scope at some point in the lifecycle. Changes in scope should be documented and appropriately authorised. The size of the change dictates the level of approval required for the change, e.g. intra-project or project sponsor.

Progress and monitoring

The sponsor and steering committee should receive regular reports on the variances against the plan and budget.

What is the relevance for due diligence?

As discussed in the overview, projects that are in progress are going to either contribute to the value of the company or detract from it.

However, we are not just assessing whether the project is on time and to budget but also whether it will add value to the post-deal organisation. So we need to assess the project with one eye on the future.

We discussed previously whether the project infrastructure is in line with the IT strategy and business strategy of the new organisation.

The costs of abandoning the project also need to be considered including ending contracts early with suppliers and vendors countered by savings of contractors no longer being required.

How to audit projects in progress

Objective

To assess projects in progress to assess the likelihood of success and whether the deliverable is fit for purpose for the new organisation.

Risk

The target organisation is spending money on a project destined to fail.

The project deliverable is not fit for purpose for the new organisation.

Audit steps

By enquiry and reviewing documentation understand how the project is managed and governed including the:

- business case.
- business requirements.
- project plan.
- project reporting.

Enquire with the future management to understand the IT and business strategy and discuss with them the project in question.

We then make a judgement considering all the preceding factors as to whether the project will add value or detract value from the target organisation.

Summary and key take-aways

We have seen that projects in progress can add value to the target organisation or detract from it. The assessment of whether the project will add value to the new organisation and whether it is appropriately managed in the target organisation requires us to meet with both the target's management and the management of the new organisation.

We need to understand the context of the project, its progress and whether the project is likely to be a success in the target organisation and assess whether it is going to deliver a system that is fit for purpose in the new organisation.

CHAPTER 7: IT SERVICE PROVISION AND VALUE FOR MONEY

Overview

Our due diligence project is progressing well and we have completed most of the things auditors are in their comfort zone reporting on. Now we come to something we need to make a judgement on: value for money (vfm) of IT service provision.

Here we review:

- whether there has been adequate investment in IT.
- the capability and cost of the IT team.
- the licensing terms of the IT being transferred.
- the key third-party service providers.

In some respects vfm of IT is relatively straightforward when looking at the IT investment and IT team and it is very easy to overcomplicate the work.

The investment in IT we can almost say is visible. Visit the data centre and look at the hardware. If it is recent equipment, it is an indication of either regular investment or a catch-up investment due to a prior lack.

The second visit is to the data room to review the IT strategy, IT budgets and actual expenditure for the last five years if the IT is in-house. Alternatively look at the contract with the outsource service provider and what is to be replaced and renewed over the life of the contract. Note how far through the contract we are.

Organisations such as Gartner also provide a wealth of benchmarks about IT expenditure, both operating cost and capital expenditure, which is always useful. We discuss the danger of benchmarks later.

Assessing the IT team can be a very difficult exercise unless we have a very good working relationship because we are helping to decide the future of the team. We need to identify key members of the team essential to keeping the IT operational and those who make up the numbers.

Again, there are many benchmarks available for looking at, e.g. IT staff per hundred employees, and this generic ratio is broken down into each of the IT functions. We emphasise the risks of using benchmarks.

There is also a lot of data available to look at the cost of the IT team per head.

However, we also have to look at the capability of the team in total and the individuals themselves. A starting point is to see if the individuals have explicit and detailed job descriptions against which they can be measured. Then have a look, keeping the data confidential, at the ratings issued following the most recent appraisals. Assuming there is a staff appraisal system.

The next part of the vfm review takes us back into our comfort zone looking at what IT assets are being transferred to the new organisation. Indeed, are the assets transferrable? Who actually own the assets? Who owns the licences for software? And do the terms of the licence allow transfer?

The risks of using benchmarks are that the benchmark must be appropriate for the organisation. There is no point using a benchmark appropriate for a FTSE 100 company on an SME company because it gives misleading information about the IT expenditure and IT team. The data for the organisation's direct peer group and industry has to be available to make benchmarking valuable.

Investment in IT

As we discussed in the Overview the first thing to do to assess whether the investment in IT is adequate is to visit the data centre to view the IT hardware (assuming you know what recent IT hardware looks like!).

Then get an inventory of the IT including:

- the purchase dates and model numbers of hardware.
- the version number, purchase date and implementation date of software.

Also have a look at the help desk statistics and see what the numbers of issues are per system and the resolution time. These should be available in the data room. A high number of issues are an indication that the IT estate is old and unreliable.

While we are in the data room obtain the IT strategy, IT budgets and actual expenditure for the last five years as well as any outsourcing contracts.

The key things to look for in the IT strategy are:

- The date the IT strategy was issued.
- Is it a similar date to the business strategy, i.e. will the IT strategy facilitate the business strategy?

- The proposed level of expenditure.
- The proposed size of the IT team and the skills required.
- How much of the strategy has been implemented and is it on track to be achieved?

The IT budgets break down the proposed expenditure in the strategy into much more detail and include annual operating costs as well as proposed investment.

We need to appreciate the difference to the IT budget detail depending on whether the IT is hosted in-house or outsourced. For IT hosted in-house we should expect to see line items for all aspects of IT expenditure, such as equipment, software, consumables, staff and so on.

For an outsourced service provision the budget is likely to include much less detail such as the contract cost only plus any out of contract work such as projects or ad hoc work. In such situations we then need to review the contracts with the service providers to see what services and investment is included in the contract.

The actual expenditure should ideally reflect the budget, so any major fluctuations against budget could reveal emergency expenditure due to equipment failure or to fix major functionality shortcomings.

Finding such easy pickings at an outsourced service provider depends on the contract. If the company has been good at negotiating with the service provider, it is more difficult to identify emergency expenditure because it is included in normal service provision. In these cases the help desk statistics help to identify if the systems are stable.

Reviewing the outsource service provider's contract can reveal information about the IT investment. There may be a stipulation that the organisation has to upgrade to a specific model of hardware and version of software at the start of the contract. This could be because the IT estate was old and the service provider did not have the skills and tools to manage the IT estate.

We normally find that where the IT is outsourced the subject of the due diligence exercise is kept up to date or maybe a couple of versions behind the latest available to avoid untested functionality!

Benchmarking the costs of IT and the IT investment can provide a valuable insight into how the organisation has managed IT investment and its cost base. As discussed previously, to make benchmarks usable the data of the peer group and industry has to be available. If this is available, the benchmarks we look for are:

- IT capital expenditure per unit of revenue.
- IT operational expenditure per unit of revenue.
- IT operational expenditure per unit of total operating costs.
- IT outsource expenditure per £k total operating costs.

Any major variances against the peer group require explaining.

The capability and cost of the IT team

The IT team morale is likely to be low before and during the due diligence exercise and people may be tempted to leave. We need to quickly identify if there are any key people that need to be retained. In certain circumstances 'golden handcuffs' payments may be required with either old technology or very advanced technology where skills are scarce.

How do we start reviewing the IT team? Meeting with the chief information officer (CIO) to understand the team, how it operates, the technology involved and the skills of the CIO is vital to the review. Question the CIO about the stability of the team and the frequency of leavers and joiners.

In the data room see if there are explicit job descriptions for every member of the IT team. If there are people and change consultants working on the due diligence exercise, it may be valuable to get them to look at the job descriptions to see if they are suitable and appropriate, i.e. are they measurable in a performance management process? The people and change consultants can also give us their view on how effective the performance management process is.

Having ascertained the quality of the job descriptions and the performance management process, request the most recent statistics from the performance process to see how many high flyers and poor performers are in the team.

If the IT team has conducted satisfaction surveys in the user community, these can also provide an insight into the performance of the IT team.

Earlier in the process we looked at the help desk statistics and these can give an equally valuable insight into the capability of the IT team. Look at the nature of the issues logged. For issues that we are familiar with and know how long resolution should take, see if this team took a similar time. Significantly longer times could indicate a skills deficit.

Also look for the same issue recurring regularly. If the technology is relatively up-to-date, again a skills deficit may be the underlying issue.

Evidence of skills shortages leads nicely into training. Does the organisation regularly train the team? Look for evidence of people being regularly trained and formal training programmes. If people have qualifications, look for evidence that they are maintaining their professional development.

The cost of the IT team is something we can assess and get some relevant benchmark material on relatively easily. Salary and benefit data for IT skills is available from many sources. If there are significant variances, explanations are required. For example, a DBA (database administrator) paid in excess of the normal market rate may indicate that skills are scarce for old technology.

Other benchmarks we look at, assuming direct peer group data is available, are:

- Number of employees per IT staff, then break this down into:
  - level one support
  - level two support
  - level three support
  - specific application support staff per number of users

- o specific hardware support staff per number of users.
- IT staff cost per employee.
- IT staff in sourced versus contractor.
- Distribution of IT staff by IT function and technology domain.

Significant variances to the peer group can indicate underlying issues in the technology, so seek clarification of the variance. Having established the cost and capability of the IT team, we need to discuss with the management of the new organisation who and what package is to be TUPE-ed (Transfer of Undertakings (Protection of Employment)) over.

Transfer of assets and licensing

We are nearing the end of our review and have concluded we are relatively satisfied with the technology and the IT team. Now we need to investigate exactly which assets are being transferred to the new organisation.

This is where our lives become really interesting! In the data room we have the inventory of assets and those that are being transferred are highlighted, but who owns them?

We need to seek evidence that the subject of the due diligence actually owns the hardware and applications being transferred. If we are looking at a disposal from a large group, establishing the ownership of assets can be challenging to say the least. Assets are often transferred around the group without detailed tracking.

Additional help from data analytics colleagues may be necessary to forensically track assets around the group to establish where the ownership lies. If the ownership is all within the organisation that is the subject of the due diligence then the financial aspects of the transfer should be relatively simple.

However, if the assets are owned elsewhere in the group, we need to establish what the cost is going to be to the subject of the due diligence to acquire ownership. We work with the wider due diligence team here because some hard negotiating may be necessary.

Now we enter the quagmire of licensing of operating systems, middleware and applications. The terms and conditions of licences are as variable as the wind! We will probably have to work with an IT lawyer to understand all the terms and conditions of the licences and the ability to transfer them to the new organisation.

Before transferring we also need to establish the number of licences we require to operate the business effectively and efficiently. Organisations rarely look at the cost of licensing properly and invariably purchase more licences than are actually required. We want to avoid unnecessary cost.

Again, there may be a significant cost involved with either transferring licences or obtaining new licences.

Outsourced service providers are likely to own certainly the hardware and may also provide the software on a software as a service basis. In such situations we need to ascertain the cost for the new organisation of arranging a transition period and cost with them to enable the new organisation to continue business until its own arrangements are in place.

In most cases the deal is likely to be concluded long before any assets are physically transferred and we need a transition period to enable us to transfer the assets in an orderly manner or replace the assets and to enable the new organisation to continue business. This, again, can be a significant cost that needs to be accounted for in the deal.

Key third-party service providers

We have looked at the use of outsource service providers throughout the chapter; however, we also need to identify the service providers key to the transaction.

There are two methods we use to identify the key service providers. In *Chapter 3* we looked at identifying the key systems and how we do that; we use a similar method to identify the key service providers.

The business process documentation we created to identify the key systems also holds the key to identifying the key service providers. As we document the key business processes the interface with the key service providers is also identified.

Confirmation of the key service providers is confirmed by the second method of identifying the key service providers. Here we look at the expenditure of the service providers.

We continue to find outsource contracts that do not provide value for money. Organisations agree contracts with service providers without sufficient legal advice, leading to higher fees rather than providing value for money. For example, a low monthly fee is agreed but any emergency or extraordinary services are charged at a very high rate.

Auditing IT service provision value for money

Objectives:

- Has there been adequate investment in IT?
- Assessing the capability and cost of the IT team.
- Assessing third-party service providers as to their service provision, cost and value for money.
- Establishing the assets to be transferred and the licensing terms of the IT being transferred.

Audit risks

We make an incorrect assessment of all three elements in the objectives and impose additional costs on the new organisation.

Poor-quality data leads to an incorrect assessment.

Audit approach

The ability to provide advice that adds value to the deal is restricted by the quality of the data available. As auditors we can make a qualitative judgement on the quality of the data available. If we decide it is poor quality, we need to request the organisation to provide what is required to make our Summary and key take-aways.

The auditor should ascertain the following by enquiry and observation:

- The efficacy of the IT strategy, its proposed cost, whether it supports the business strategy and how complete the implementation is.
- The completeness and accuracy of the IT budget and how the actual expenditure compares.
- The cost of outsourced service provision.
- Review the IT inventory to establish how old the IT estate is.
- The size and cost of the IT team.
- How well defined the roles and responsibilities of the team are.
- The performance of the IT team by understanding the latest performance review statistics and any satisfaction surveys conducted.
- Establish what assets are to be transferred to the new organisation.

Then through analysis, which might include benchmarking, establish:

- Whether the investment in IT is in line with the industry and peer group.
- Whether the IT team is capable and who should be retained in the new organisation.
- The cost of transferring the assets and whether they can be transferred.

- The investment required for any shortfall caused by old technology, lack of skills or the inability to transfer assets.
- What licences, how many and at what cost are going to be transferred to the new organisation.

Summary and key take-aways

We have established the value of the IT, the capability of the IT team and what assets are to be transferred.

In assessing the investment and cost of IT we have seen that our auditing skills are utilised to understand the cost base and whether the investment is providing value or not. In completing this assessment the careful use of benchmarking can provide a valuable insight as long as it is conducted using directly comparable data, i.e. the organisation's peer group.

The ownership of the assets and their licensing has been known to cause deals to be abandoned – it can be that impossible to solve. In large groups we are likely to work with forensic data analysts to track assets around the group to establish ownership. With licensing our friends are likely to be the IT lawyer who makes the decision on whether licences can be transferred legally and at what cost.

Minimising the number of licences the new organisation requires to operate efficiently and effectively is also part of the due diligence exercise.

In addition we have looked at the transition arrangements that are likely to be required plus working with the wider due diligence team to negotiate the cost of the transition arrangements.

CHAPTER 8: REPORTING IT DUE DILIGENCE ASSIGNMENTS

Overview

Having completed the hard work of reviewing IT issues for the due diligence assignment, it is now important to present these findings in a way that have an impact on the stakeholders. In this chapter we consider the following specific issues relating to due diligence reporting:

- specific IT due diligence reporting.
- checklist of issues to include.

Specific IT due diligence reporting

It is very rare that a due diligence review only consists of IT due diligence. Usually the work of the IT specialist is incorporated into the whole review and reporting. We have seen cases where the IT specialist has just written a report in their own standard style. Given the tight timelines and need for consistency this is not a good option. If the drafting is left to a non-IT specialist, wordings may be changed, inadvertently changing the meaning. This happened to us once and the report stated the exact opposite of what was intended – luckily the error was identified during the report review QA process! It is better if the IT specialist does the initial drafting. This requires an understanding of the special circumstances for due diligence reports.

There are three issues to consider when writing an IT due diligence report:

1. Consider the audience/stakeholders. They are probably not from an IT background but still need to grasp the key implications of your findings and recommendations.

2. Remember the objectives for your review. Any additional information may be irrelevant and cause confusion.

3. Ensure the report is structured well and will be easy to reference later.

Target audience

The final report, including all aspects of due diligence, is likely to be long. Most of the audience are likely to be focused on non-IT issues. It is therefore important to make a strong impact, for example by:

- ensuring you understand the reporting requirements and style required.

- being succinct and to the point.

- avoiding the use of technical jargon or acronyms.

- keep to the facts and be clear where you are expressing an opinion.

- use diagrams and tables effectively in the body of the text and appendices to provide detailed information if required.

- applying the 'So what?' test to ensure the understanding of a lay reader.

- clearly stating the impact of findings on bid viability or hidden opportunities, price or other negotiating points, and post-merger implications.

Review, re-review and then review again.

Objectives of the report

We saw in earlier chapters that it is important to have clearly understood the objectives of the review. These should drive, and be the focus of, the report. If we are working for the seller, we may have disclosure requirements about revealing key issues, but the main objective of the report is to assist in the deal. To be specific:

- If writing for the buyer – want to maximise the return on the deal.
- If writing for the seller – want to get the best/ maximum value from the deal.

Whomever we are writing for, our objective is to ensure any relevant, key IT issues are clearly communicated and that their consequences for the deal are understood and actioned. We also need to show that we have addressed all the objectives agreed for our review and reach conclusions on each, making clear deal and/or post-deal recommendations.

Report structure

Some colleagues have joked that we seem to write the report before starting the work. Although this is not true, we find it useful to understand the reporting requirements before we start a review. This ensures a focus throughout the review. The structure, style and content of the due diligence report are more formal than for other types of report. A typical structure for an IT due diligence section may be:

- Objectives of review
- Executive summary and Summary and key take-aways
- Key findings (see below)
- Recommendations.

Appendices of supporting information

CHAPTER 9: POST-DUE-DILIGENCE

Overview and introduction to post-merger integration

IBM (see *damachicago.org/wp-content/uploads/2012/01/ IBM-DAMA-Feb-2012.pdf*) states that "$2 of every $5 of merger synergy comes from IT."

Realisation of the benefits from the deal can only be achieved if the post-merger integration process is successful. The degree of integration depends on the objectives for the deal, e.g. it may be that the acquirer wishes not to fully integrate the new business so that it can be sold on at a later stage. In most cases, however, it is likely that integration, either fully or partially, is required.

Hard evidence is difficult to obtain; however, there are estimates that only 30–50% of mergers and acquisitions actually achieve the business benefits identified during due diligence. This is mainly due to post-merger integration issues, which may be cultural, due to different management styles, but could also be technical where the costs of integration are higher than expected. If the takeover was hostile, there could be significant repercussions in the attitude of management and this may also impact the likelihood of a successful merger.

While all of this happening there is still a business to run – sales to be made, customers to be served and financial reporting/compliance to continue.

There has been a great deal of academic research based on acquisitions by GE and others. Based on this research, the following principles have been postulated for PMI (Post Merger Integration):

- PMI should start even before the merger process is instituted or at the due diligence stage.
- PMIs need to be tailored to suit the needs of each combination.
- PMI processes should have effective leaders and managers.
- PMI is not just a matter of harmonizing procedures, physical equipment, financial and legal matters. It is a matter of bringing people from differing cultures to work together in harmony. Melding cultures is important if a merger is to be a success.
- PMI works best when done in a transparent and open environment – meaning communication is done effectively and honestly as truth is valued.
- Speed in implementation of PMI is vital in ensuring merger success.

Teng, Michael (2012-06-23). *Post-Merger Integration: Improving shareholders' values after a merger* (Kindle Locations 561–566). Kindle Edition.

Often where the deal is a larger organisation taking over a much smaller one, the failure of post-integration relates primarily to system integration features. Owners of small businesses can rely on informal processes to meet their objectives; these are less practical or acceptable for the new business. The IT review team should be able to assist with identifying these potential issues and ways of integrating systems. For example, we heard of a case recently where there was a particular failure of systems and communication. In the motor industry the purchasing systems were not integrated following a merger – as a result important components were not ordered and open invoices were not paid. Both purchasing departments reacted to the issue – and the following week all invoices were paid twice over!

Further information

Data auditing tools:

www.infotech.com/research/ss/integrate-a-data-audit-into-the-data-management-plan

ITG RESOURCES

IT Governance Ltd sources, creates and delivers products and services to meet the real-world, evolving IT governance needs of today's organisations, directors, managers and practitioners.

The ITG website (*www.itgovernance.co.uk*) is the international one-stop-shop for corporate and IT governance information, advice, guidance, books, tools, training and consultancy.

Publishing Services

IT Governance Publishing (ITGP) is the world's leading IT-GRC publishing imprint that is wholly owned by IT Governance Ltd.

With books and tools covering all IT governance, risk and compliance frameworks, we are the publisher of choice for authors and distributors alike, producing unique and practical publications of the highest quality, in the latest formats available, which readers will find invaluable.

www.itgovernancepublishing.co.uk is the website dedicated to ITGP. Other titles published by ITGP that may be of interest include:

- Data Protection Compliance in the UK

  www.itgovernance.co.uk/shop/p-515-data-protection-compliance-in-the-uk.aspx

- Agile Governance and Audit

  www.itgovernance.co.uk/shop/p-1616-agile-governance-and-audit.aspx.

We also offer a range of off-the-shelf *toolkits* that give comprehensive, customisable documents to help users create the specific documentation they need to properly implement a management system or standard. Written by experienced practitioners and based on the latest best practice, ITGP toolkits can save months of work for organisations working towards compliance with a given standard.

To see the full range of toolkits available please see:

www.itgovernance.co.uk/shop/c-129-toolkits.aspx.

Books and tools published by IT Governance Publishing (ITGP) are available from all business booksellers and the following websites:

www.itgovernance.eu   *www.itgovernanceusa.com*

www.itgovernance.in   *www.itgovernancesa.co.za*

www.itgovernance.asia.

Training Services

The IT due diligence process depends on determining the adequacy of your information security systems. The implementation, maintenance and continual improvement of those systems depends on appropriate training. ISO27001 is the international standard for information security management; IT Governance's ISO27001 Learning Pathway provides information security courses from Foundation to Advanced level, with qualifications awarded by IBITGQ.

The ISO27001 Learning Pathway comprises the following courses:

- Foundation level
  - ISO27001 Certified ISMS Foundation course

- o ISO27001 Certified Internal Auditor course
- o Information Security Foundation based on ISO27002 course.
- Advanced level
  - o ISO27001 Certified ISMS Lead Implementer Masterclass
  - o ISO 27001 Certified ISMS Lead Auditor course
  - o ISO27005 Certified ISMS Risk Management course
  - o ISO 27001:2013 ISMS Certified Transition course.

Many courses are available in Live Online as well as classroom formats, so delegates can learn and achieve essential career progression from the comfort of their own homes and offices.

Delegates passing the exams associated with our ISO27001 Learning Pathway will gain qualifications from IBITGQ, including CIS F, CIS IA, CIS LI, CIS LA, CIS RM and CIS 2013 UP).

IT Governance is an acknowledged leader in the world of ISO27001 and information security management training. Our practical, hands-on approach is delivered by experienced practitioners, who focus on improving your knowledge, developing your skills, and awarding relevant, industry-recognised certifications. Our fully integrated and structured learning paths accommodate delegates with various levels of knowledge, and our courses can be delivered in a variety of formats to suit all delegates.

For more information about IT Governance's ISO 27001 learning pathway, please see: *www.itgovernance.co.uk/ iso27001-information-security-training.aspx*.

For information on any of our many other courses, including PCI DSS compliance, business continuity, IT governance, service management and professional certification courses, please see: *www.itgovernance.co.uk/training.aspx*.

Professional Services and Consultancy

The IT due diligence process depends on determining the adequacy of your information security systems. Whether you're certified to an international standard such as ISO27001, use a methodology like PRINCE2® or COBIT®, or follow your own processes, good security depends on regular penetration testing to determine – and mitigate – the vulnerabilities you present to the Internet.

IT Governance's consultant-driven penetration tests combine a range of advanced manual tests by our expert, CREST-accredited penetration testers with a number of automated vulnerability scans, using multiple tools and techniques, to enable you to protect your web applications from malicious attack.

Our Web Application Penetration Test can include:

- a detailed consultation session to identify the depth and breadth of the tests required.
- careful scoping of the test environment to establish the exact extent of the testing exercise (internal or external) dependent on your needs.
- a range of manual tests conducted by our team of highly skilled penetration testers using a methodology closely aligned with the OWASP methodology.
- a series of automated vulnerability scans.
- immediate notification of identified critical vulnerabilities so that you can take remedial action as soon as possible.

- a detailed technical report that details the identified vulnerabilities, ranked in order of significance.
- a list of recommended countermeasures to address any identified vulnerabilities.
- an executive summary for your management team that explains in business terms what the risks mean.

IT Governance's expert consultants have over a decade's practical experience, having worked on numerous successful projects around the world with organisations of all sizes, sectors and locations, from small organisations to multinationals.

As a CREST member company, IT Governance has been verified as meeting rigorous standards of security testing. Our clients can rest assured that our technical work will be carried out by qualified and knowledgeable professionals.

For more information about penetration testing and other IT Governance technical services, please see:

www.itgovernance.co.uk/penetration-testing-packages.aspx.

Newsletter

IT governance is one of the hottest topics in business today, not least because it is also the fastest moving.

You can stay up to date with the latest developments across the whole spectrum of IT governance subject matter, including; risk management, information security, ITIL and IT service management, project governance, compliance and so much more, by subscribing to ITG's core publications and topic alert emails.

Simply visit our subscription centre and select your preferences: *www.itgovernance.co.uk/newsletter.aspx*.

EU for product safety is Stephen Evans, The Mill Enterprise Hub, Stagreenan, Drogheda, Co. Louth, A92 CD3D, Ireland. (servicecentre@itgovernance.eu)

www.ingramcontent.com/pod-product-compliance
Lightning Source LLC
Chambersburg PA
CBHW070408200326
41518CB00011B/2110

* 9 7 8 1 8 4 9 2 8 7 2 0 3 *